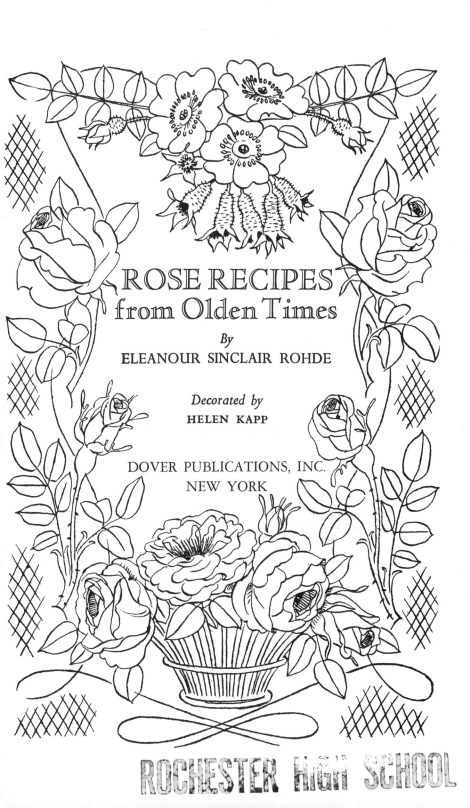

# ROSE RECIPES
## from Olden Times

*By*
ELEANOUR SINCLAIR ROHDE

*Decorated by*
HELEN KAPP

DOVER PUBLICATIONS, INC.
NEW YORK

This Dover edition, first published in 1973, is an
unabridged and unaltered republication of the work
first published by Routledge in 1939 under the title
*Rose Recipes*.

*International Standard Book Number: 0-486-22957-2*
*Library of Congress Catalog Card Number: 73-78369*

Manufactured in the United States of America
Dover Publications, Inc.
180 Varick Street
New York, N. Y. 10014

*To*
*Anne*
*with love from*
*E.S.R.*

# CONTENTS

# DETAILED CONTENTS

## POT-POURRIS, SWEET BAGS, AND POMANDERS

## PERFUMES AND SWEET WATERS

## CULINARY RECIPES

xiii

# INTRODUCTION

# INTRODUCTION

IN THE days when Roses were valued more for their fragrance, sweet flavour, and medicinal virtues than for their beauty the petals were used in countless ways. Most folk associate flower recipes with old vellum-bound volumes and regard the recipes therein contained as being of little more than antiquarian interest. Indeed the phrase "Rose recipes" conjures up visions of sixteenth and seventeenth century still rooms, busy housewives and attendant maids in picturesque costumes bringing in great baskets of freshly gathered Roses. It is true that many of the old recipes or "receipts" as the word was more commonly spelt are too complicated for these hurried times but many are simple and practical.

Even in the days of our great-grandmothers to whom Roses

were of less account than to their forebears these flowers were used for many delightful confections. They made syrups, jellies and conserves of Roses, they crystallized the petals, they flavoured sugar with Roses, they made fresh rose-water to wash their hands, they preserved rose-buds in order to have freshly blown Roses in mid-winter, honey of roses and rose lozenges were favourite confections, the wealthy made Rossoly and Roset, snuff was scented with Musk roses, little bags of dried rose petals were laid among fine linen, powdered petals were incorporated in home-made candles, rose petals predominated in pot-pourris and sweet bags, wine and vinegar were flavoured with Roses, in perfumes and sweet water Roses were usually the chief ingredients and rose petals were used medicinally in many ways.

Think of the millions of roses wasted every year in these islands! What our ancestors would have thought of such waste it is difficult to imagine. Pot-pourris are still however almost universally appreciated, sweet bags might well be revived, there are many dainty rose confections that even the busy modern housewife can find time to make and some of the rose cosmetics are delightful to use.

For many of the recipes dried or powdered rose petals are required and as with all flowers the way they are gathered and dried makes a great difference. They should be gathered when the dew has dried off them but before the sun is at its height. The slowest and most unsatisfactory way of drying them is to spread the petals out on a table: the best way is to spread them out on large wire sieves of the type used in confectioners' shops. Flowers to be dried should not be exposed to

18

sunlight. By using sieves the air circulates all round the petals and consequently they dry more quickly. It is essential to use sieves with a small mesh, otherwise the petals as they dry are apt to fall through. Netting fastened to a wooden frame is an admirable substitute for a sieve. When perfectly dry the petals should be rubbed to powder and stored in closely stoppered bottles. If exposed to the atmosphere for long, especially in winter, the petals naturally absorb moisture and soon become useless.

Dried rose petals figured largely in the old sweet bags used not merely for scenting linen but to hang on wing arm-chairs. The mixture of dried Rose petals, mint leaves and powdered cloves recommended in Rams Little Dodeon (1606) has a most pleasing fragrance. You are recommended to "take it to bed with you and it will cause you to sleep and it is good to smell unto at other times". Musk was formerly more popular than it is now and it figures in many recipes for sweet bags. I have given various representative sweet bag recipes and it will be noted that in the nineteenth century housewives once more favoured the simpler recipes.

In Elizabethan times they dried petals whole in sand and I have frequently done this. Unlike petals dried in the ordinary way those dried in sand come out scarcely wrinkled and a far better colour. Roses, Carnations, Marigolds, etc., can all be dried this way and a bowl of them in varied colours is charmingly decorative in winter. I use large empty stationery boxes, spreading a layer of sand and a layer of petals altern- ately. Of course no lid must be put on or the moisture could not escape. I stand the boxes in a hot linen cupboard for quite a week and by that time the petals are perfectly dry. The petals should be stored in airtight tins or stoppered bottles till wanted. In winter the petals keep dry and absorb no moisture if the bowls containing them are stood near hot pipes. I have quoted various recipes for drying rose petals but in my experience this is the best way.

For drying roses in the ordinary way, i.e. in the shade in a room, I think the most practical method is to have stands about ten feet high with canvas "shelves" at intervals of a foot all the way up. If the "shelves" measure four feet each way this gives an area of 160 square feet to each stand. If flowers and leaves are gathered all through the season they can be cleared as soon as powder-dry and stored till mixing time. Some people prefer to dry in a draught and in this case pieces of butter muslin are useful to throw over the shelves to prevent the petals, etc., being blown away.

Pot-pourris may be roughly divided into two groups—those that consist merely of dried flowers and have therefore a faint perfume and those that are more richly scented by adding essential oils, etc. The pot-pourris commonly sold are usually sprayed with a mixture of perfumes and when these have evaporated the scent of the pot-pourri is scarcely noticeable. Personally I far prefer the soft delicate scent of a pot-pourri that consists solely of dried flowers and aromatic leaves with perhaps the addition of a little orris, allspice, etc. The leaves of the Rose Geranium, Rose root (Sedum rhodiola), the scent of which is almost indistinguishable from the scent of old roses such as the Apothecary's rose, Lemon Verbena, Sweet Briar, Honeysuckles, Philadephus, Heliotrope or

Cherry Pie as it is more commonly called, Carnations and Pinks, Woodruff, the scent of which when dried resembles new mown hay, and a few of the sweet herbs such as Lavender, Southernwood (sometimes known as Lad's Love or Old Man), Balm, Rosemary, Sweet Marjoram, Mints, etc., are amongst the best ingredients for a pot-pourri. For those who like a spicy pot-pourri, powdered Coriander Cloves and Allspice can be added. A little sandal wood is also pleasant, but should not be overdone. Meadowsweet is not commonly dried for pot-pourri nowadays nor is its scent much appreciated, but we have Parkinson's authority for it that it was Queen Elizabeth's favourite stewing herb.

What we call moist pot-pourris were formerly called by the prettier name of scent jars. Instead of the modern labour-saving method of spraying the flowers with various essences, such as essence of Rosemary, oil of cloves, eau de Cologne, essence of Verbena, Rosewater, essence of Heliotrope, oil of cinnamon, etc., the flowers were more or less pickled. Pot-pourris of this kind were made in deep big crocks and the proportions were about half a pound of bay salt and a handful of coarse kitchen salt to two pounds of flowers. The petals and salts were strewn in layers about half an inch thick and on top was placed a wooden lid with a weight on it to keep the whole well pressed down. After a week the mixture was spread out to dry but not in the sun. Then the dried leaves such as Verbena, Rosemary, Lavender, etc., were added. Last of all the spices were added, usually bruised cloves, powdered All-spice, Coriander, Cinnamon broken in small pieces allowing two or three ounces of spices to every pound of the pickle. For

21

*six weeks the whole was stored in an airtight jar, after which a few drops of some essential oil were added.*

Roses, however, were the chief ingredients in all pot-pourris, and the roses chiefly valued for pot-pourris were the Apothecary's Rose (R. officinalis), the Cabbage Rose, and most of the centifolia hybrids, R. gallica, Kazanlik (the rose grown in Bulgaria for attar of roses), Damask roses, the most sweetly scented of the rugosa hybrids, the Bourbon roses, notably Madame Isaac Pereire and Parfum de l'Haye. To these may be added George Dickson, Gruss an Teiplitz, Chateau de Clos Vougeout, Mrs. John Laing.

Of all sweet waters to wash in the pleasantest is I think freshly made rose water. It smells, not of roses, but of pot-pourri of roses. Most wash-stands in Victorian times included a small dainty basin and equally diminutive jug. In country houses these were commonly used for rose water. Twentieth century guests are as appreciative as those of the last century when they find a small jug of freshly made rose water awaiting them. And making this fragrant water takes only a few minutes and costs nothing beyond the trouble of gathering the roses. Gather about two pounds of scented petals before they fall, put them in a lined saucepan or preferably an earthenware pan and just cover with cold water preferably soft water. Bring slowly almost to the boil, then leave till cold and strain off the water. If only dark red roses are used the water is a very pale pink, but roses of other colours turn the water a brownish-yellow. In any case the water is faintly but deliciously fragrant for quite two days. Rose water made from deep red scented roses is I think the best. Rose vinegar which fastidious French women use to allay headaches is very simple to make. A jar of the best white wine vinegar is half filled with rose petals and these are left to steep for twenty-four hours, preferably in the sun, and then strained off. A handkerchief dipped in rose vinegar laid on the forehead is most cooling and refreshing.

Roses shed their petals unheeded nowadays, but in olden times they were carefully garnered day by day and dried. Powdered rose petals can be used in many ways. They make, for instance, a pretty decoration for junkets, custards, etc. Fresh rose petals finely chopped and mixed with other edible flowers such as nasturtiums, borage, carnations, marigolds, etc., are a most pleasing addition to a salad for the flavour is unusual and the mixture of colours of the finely chopped petals looks gay. Rose petal sandwiches were a favourite dainty for tea in Victorian times. Dark red roses are the best to use for this purpose with very thinly cut brown bread and butter. Home-made bread and real country butter or thick cream are of course the ideal. The rose and fruit salad described on page 81 sounds a curious mixture, but it is very good.

Sugar flavoured with roses was evidently very popular in olden times, for recipes for this confection figure in almost every sixteenth and seventeenth century cookery book. It is a slow process for it is made by pounding white sugar with double its weight of rose petals. Candied or preserved rose petals are amongst the daintiest sweets and the easiest way of preserving them is with white of egg. The process is simple, but requires dainty fingers and leisure. The whites of the

23

eggs to be used should be beaten but not to a stiff froth, and then with a clean new paint brush each petal should be coated on both sides. Then spread out the petals carefully on a large dish and powder with castor sugar. Turn each petal separately and dust the other sides with sugar. Choose a hot summer day for this candying for the roses should be dried in the sun for about an hour. When quite dry and crisp arrange the petals in layers in an airtight tin, putting stiff white paper between each layer of petals.

Rose petal conserve and jelly are confections fit for Titania and should be served in the daintiest jars. In some recipes fresh petals are used and in others dried rose petals. The rose flavour is strongest if dried petals are used, and of course the roses used must be scented kinds. Roses have a very astringent flavour and it will be noted that in all recipes a large quantity of sugar is used, in proportion to the quantity of rose petals.

Even our wild roses were not wasted formerly. Tea was made from the leaves (not petals) of the dog rose. Conserve of rose hips was esteemed as a delicacy and in Queen Victoria's time was frequently served at Balmoral Castle. Flavoured with lemon juice, ginger and cinnamon to taste, it makes an uncommon filling for pastry tartlets.

Few take the trouble nowadays to preserve rose-buds to open in mid-winter, for modern hybrid roses frequently flower well into December. In bleak parts, however, it is worth preserving at least a few so as to have roses at Christmas time. To secure flowers in the depth of winter, gather rose-buds that are just showing colour, on a dry day and when the dew has dried off them. Cut them with a sharp knife and select those with long stems. This is important for short stemmed specimens are not likely to prove satisfactory. As each stem is cut dip it at once in soft wax. When the wax on all the stems has set, wrap the roses separately in tissue paper and pack them carefully in a box, preferably a wooden box. Put the box in a dry but cool place and if possible in an even temperature. A temperature of about forty-five to fifty degrees is ideal and in any case the place must be frost proof but not warm. When wanted unpack the rose-buds, cut off the waxed ends and put the stems in water, that is just tepid. The buds will open very gradually. Even in mediæval times it was customary to preserve roses to have them in flower in mid-winter. The earliest recipe for this purpose that I know is in Le Menagier de Paris, that charming treatise written by a fourteenth century bourgeois of Paris for his young wife. In the book he states that she had begged him not to reprove her when guests were present for her mistakes, but to wait until they were alone together. Consequently he wrote this treatise, the first part of which consists of moral precepts and the second of the ordering of a bourgeois house and garden. In the section on gardening he gives the method of preserving roses by picking them in bud, enclosing them in a tube of wood, sealing them up and then leaving the tube weighted with a stone in running water until the flowers were wanted. It is pleasant to visualize the young wife in the elaborate costume of the period diligently carrying out all her husband's elaborate instructions.

Indeed no small measure of the charm that attaches to old

recipes is, I think, the personality of the writers. Many of the rose recipes I have quoted were written by people whose names were in their day familiar if not famous. Sir Hugh Platt was one of Queen Elizabeth's courtiers, one of the noted gardeners of his time, and a recognized authority on soils. His most attractive book is a tiny volume entitled Delights for Ladies, which went through numerous editions. Every page is surrounded with a design of roses, violets, marigolds and gilliflowers with E.R. (the Queen's initials) interwoven. Gervase Markham, a Nottinghamshire man, who is believed to have been the first to have imported an Arab horse into this country, was a voluminous garden writer, who in his youth fought in the wars in the Low Countries and with Essex in Ireland. Mary Doggett was the wife of the founder of the competition for "Doggetts Coat and Badge" amongst the Thames watermen, a competition which still takes place every August. Sir Kenelm Digby was a man of European reputation, who numbered among his friends Ben Jonson, Galilio, Descartes, and Bacon. He was an intimate friend of Charles I and Henrietta Maria and in Charles II's reign he was one of the Council of the newly founded Royal Society. Yet this famous personality took the keenest interest in all sorts of flower recipes and in most cases he states the name of the friend who had given him the recipe. The recipes these gardeners of past times so assiduously collected transport us to a time when artificial amusements were few, especially in country parts, and when the majority of people therefore found their pleasures in the simple delights of their homes and gardens.                                        Eleanour Sinclair Rohde.

26

# POT-POURRIS, SWEET BAGS, AND
# POMANDERS

## A BAG TO SMELL UNTO, OR TO CAUSE
## ONE TO SLEEP

TAKE drie Rose leaves, keep them close in a glasse
which will keep them sweet, then take powder of
Mints, powder of Cloves in a grosse powder. Put
the same to the Rose leaves, then put all these
together in a bag, and take that to bed with you,
and it will cause you to sleepe, and it is good to
smell unto at other times.—Ram's *Little Dodoen*
1606.

## TO MAKE AN ESPECIAL SWEET POWDER
## FOR SWEET BAGS

TAKE of Red and Damask Rose-leaves of each two
ounces, of the purest Orris one pound, of Cloves
three drams, Coriander seed one dram, Cyprus
and Calamus of each halfe an ounce, Benzoin and
the Storax of each three drams; beat them all
save the Benzoin and the Storax and powder them
by themselves, then take of Muske and Civet, of
each twentie graines, mix these with a little of

29

the foresaid powder with a warm Pestle, and so little by little you may mix it with all the rest, and so with Rose leaves dried you may put it up into your sweet Bags and so keepe them seven yeares.—Sir Hugh Platt. *Delights for Ladies* 1594.

## TO MAKE SWEET POWDER FOR BAGS

TAKE of Rose leaves dryed two handfuls, of Orris four ounces, of dryed Marjarom one handful, Cloves one ounce, Benjamin two ounces, of white Sanders and yellow of each one ounce; beat all these into a gross powder, then put to it of Musk a dram, of Civet half a dram, and of Ambergreece half a dram, then put them into a Taffety Bag and use it.—Gervase Markham. *The English Housewife* 1625.

## FOR A SWEET BAG

TAKE of Damask Rose-leaves six ounces, of Orris as much, of Marjerom and sweet Basil of each an

ounce, of Cloves two ounces, yellow Sanders two
ounces, of Citron pills seven drams, of Lignum
Aloes one ounce, of Benjamin one ounce, of
Storax one ounce, of Musk one dram; bruise all
these and put them into a bag of Silk or Linnen
but silk is the best.—Gervase Markham. *The
English Housewife* 1625.

## A PERFUME FOR A SWEET BAGG

TAKE 4 pecks of Damask Rose leaves, a peck of
dryed sweet Marjerum, a pretty stick of Juniper
shaved very thin, some lemon peel dryed; half a
pound of Cypress roots, a pound of Orris, 3
quarters of a pound of Rhodium, a pound of
Coriander Seed, 3 quarters of a pound of Calamus, 3 oranges stuck with cloves, 2 ounces of
Benjamin, and an ounce of Storax. Let all these
be powdered very grossly for the first year and
immediately put into your baggs; the next year
pound and work it and it will be very good again.
—Mary Doggett. *Her Book of Receipts* 1682.

31

## SWEET SCENTED BAGS TO LAY WITH LINEN

EIGHT ounces of damask rose leaves, eight ounces of coriander seeds, eight ounces of sweet orri-root, eight ounces of calamus aromaticus, one ounce of mace, one ounce of cinnamon, half an ounce of cloves, four drachms of musk-powder, two drachms of white loaf sugar, three ounces of lavender flowers and some of Rhodium wood. Beat them well together and make them in small silk bags.—Mrs. Glasse. *The Art of Cookery* 1784.

## AN AGREEABLE SWEET-SCENTED COMPOSITION

TAKE Rose-wood six ounces, Florentine Orris a pound and a half, Calamus Aromaticus half a pound, Gum Benjamin five ounces, Cloves half an ounce, and Cinnamon an ounce; beat the whole into powder and fill your bags with it.—*The Toilet of Flora*.

32

## BAGS TO SCENT LINEN

TAKE Rose leaves dried in the shade, Cloves beat to a gross powder and Mace scraped; mix them together, and put the composition into little bags.—*The Toilet of Flora*.

## PERFUMED BAGS FOR SCENTING DRAWERS

TWO ounces of dried Rose petals, two ounce dried Lavender flowers, two ounces yellow sanders, two ounces Coriander seeds, two ounces Orris root, two ounces Calamus aromaticus, two ounces Cloves, two ounces Cinnamon bark, and one pound oak shavings. Reduce all to a coarse powder and fill linen bags with the mixture. These bags remove any musty smell from old furniture.—Nineteenth century recipe.

## RECIPE FOR POT-POURRI ASCRIBED TO LADY BLESSINGTON (1790–1845)

DRIED pale and red rose petals, one tumblerful of

lavender flowers, acacia flowers, clove gilliflowers, orange-flower petals, one wine-glassful
of mignonette flowers, one teaspoonful of heliotrope flowers, again or two of musk, 30 drops of
oil of vetivert, five drops oil of sandalwood, 10
drops oil of myrtle, 20 drops oil of jonquil. Dry the
petals and flowers, add the other ingredients and
put into a hermetically sealed jar for some time.

## DRY POT-POURRI

GATHER all the following flowers and herbs on a
fine day—Roses, Thyme, Rosemary, Sweet
Marjoram, Lavender, Myrtle, Southernwood,
Balm, Sweet Basil, Bay leaves. Dry them thor-
oughly by spreading out on sieves in the shade.
When dry rub all to powder and add at discretion
pounded cloves, a little musk and Orris root.—
A nineteenth century recipe.

## A SWEET JAR

FOUR handfulls of Damask Roses.

34

Four handfulls of Lavender flowers.
Two      ,,      ,,  Orange flowers.
   ,,      ,,      ,,  Clove Carnations.
Also the flowers of Sweet Marjoram, Thyme,
Rosemary, Myrtle and Mint of each one handful.
One Seville orange stuck with cloves well dried
and pounded, one ounce of Cinnamon and one
ounce of Cloves. The rind of two lemons, six
Bay leaves. All the ingredients must be thor-
oughly dried but not in the sun. Mix them all
together in a jar with bay salt.—Countess of
Rosse's recipe. Nineteenth century.


## A DRY POT-POURRI

TO a bason of dried scented roses add a handful of
dried knotted Marjoram, lemon thyme, Rosemary, Lavender flowers all well dried, the rind
of one lemon and one orange dried to powder,
six dried bay leaves, half an ounce of bruised
cloves, a teaspoon of Allspice. Mix well together
and stir occasionally.—Recipe. Dated 1895.

## POT-POURRI RECIPE USED BY ELEANOUR SINCLAIR ROHDE

TO a large bason of dried sweet scented rose petals allow a handful of dried lavender flowers, Rosemary, Thyme, Balm, Sweet Marjoram, Southernwood, Sweet Basil, Clove Carnations, Sweet Briar leaves, Wild Thyme, Garden Thyme, Hyssop, Philadelphus flowers, Orange flowers, Mint, Sweet Geranium leaves, Verbena, a few bruised Cloves, the dried and powdered rind of a lemon or orange, a teaspoonful of Allspice, half an ounce of Cinnamon and a good pinch of sandalwood.

Gather and dry the flowers and leaves all through the season, adding any others according to one's fancy but keeping the proportion of a bason of rose petals to a large handful of all the other ingredients put together. Store in a jar with a lid but the jar need not be air tight.

36

## SCENT JAR

REQUIRED. Sweet scented Rose petals, Lavender flowers, the petals of any other sweet scented flowers and a few bay leaves. Also $\frac{1}{2}$ lb bay salt (not bruised) $\frac{1}{2}$ lb saltpetre finely bruised with a little common salt. Sixpennyworth of storax, the same of musk and two ounces of cloves.

Gather the roses when the dew has dried off them but before the sun is at its hottest, pick off the petals and rub all flowers put into the jar with common salt. Stir all the ingredients well together and keep closely covered for a month. Stir every day. After a month has elapsed stir occasionally. Made thus the scent remains strong for many years.—A nineteenth century recipe.

## TO RENEW THE SCENT OF A POMANDER

TAKE one grain of Civet, and two of Musk, or if you double the proportion, it will be so much the sweeter; grinde them upon a stone with a little Rosewater; and after wetting your hands with

rose-water you may worke the same in your Pomander. This is a sleight to passe away an old Pomander; but my intention is honest.—Ram's *Little Dodoen* 1606.

## A POMANDER

TAKE Storax an ounce, Cloves two drammes, Benjamin halfe an ounce, Ambergreece halfe a dram, Muske fifteen graines, powder of Violets a little, incorporate them all together with Rose water.—*The Charitable Physitian* by Philbert Guibert. Esqre and Physician. Regent in Paris 1639.

## TO MAKE A POMOS LIKE THOSE THAT ARE MADE IN SPAIN

TAKE Benjamin half a pound, steep it in rose-water, expose it to the sun the space of six weeks, stirring it three or four times a day; and when you see that it groweth dry add still more Rose-water

38

to it. Then grinde it well with four Cloves and a little Cinnamon in powder, and one ounce of Storax, half an ounce of Ambergris, a quarter of an ounce of Civet, half an ounce of the perfumed Italian powder, one ounce of Rose powder, a dram of Musk; boyle this together in as much Rosewater as will just cover it till it be well incorporated together. This proportion will serve for eight Pomos.—Sir Kenelm Digby. *Choice and Experimented Receipts* 1668.

## A POMANDER

TAKE a quarter of an ounce of Civit, a quarter and a half quarter of an ounce of Ambergreese, not half a quarter of an ounce of ye spiritt of Roses, 7 ounces of Benjamin, allmost a pound of Damask Rose-buds cutt. Lay gumdragon on rose water and with it make up your Pomander, with beads as big as nutmegs; when you make them up wash your hands with oyle of Jasmin to smooth them, then make them have a gloss; this quantity will

make seaven braceletes.—Mary Doggett. *Her Book of Receipts* 1682.

## HOW TO DRY ROSE LEAVES, OR ANY OTHER SINGLE FLOWERS WITHOUT WRINKLING

IF you would performe the same wel in rose leaves, you must in rose time make a choice of such roses as are neither in the bud, nor full blowne (for these have the smoothest leaves of all other) which you must especially cull and chuse from the rest; then take sand, wash it in some change of waters, drie it thoroughly well, either in an oven, or in the sunne; and having shallow square or long boxes of four five or six inches deepe, make first an even lay of sand in the bottom upon which lay your rose leaves, one by one (so as none of the touch other) till you have covered all the sand, then strow sand upon thos leaves till you have thinly covered them all, and then make another laie of leaves as before, and so

40

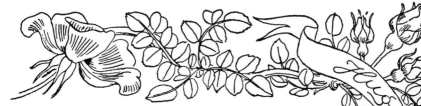

lay upon lay etc., Set this box in some warme
place in a hot sunny day (and commonly in two
hot sunny dayes they will be thorow dry) then
take them out carefully with your hand without
breaking. Keepe these leaves in jarre glasses,
bound about with paper neere a chimney, or
stove, for feare of relenting. I finde the red Rose
leafe best to be kept in this manner; also take
away the stalks of pansies, stock gilliflowers or
other single flowers; pricke them one by one in
sand, pressing downe theire leaves smooth with
more sand laid evenly upon them. And thus you
may have Rose leaves and other flowers to lay
about your basons, windows, etc., all the winter
long. Also this secret is very requisite for a good
simplifier, because hee may dry the leaf of any
herb in this manner; and lay it being dry in his
herbal with the simple which it representeth,
whereby he may easily learne to know the names
of all simples which he desireth.—Sir Hugh
Platt. *Delights for Ladies* 1594.

41

## HOW TO DRY ROSE LEAVES IN A MOST
## EXCELLENT MANNER

WHEN you have newly taken out your bread, then
put in your Roses in a sieve, first clipping away
the whites that they may be all of one colour, lay
them about one inch in thickness in the sieve;
and when they have stood halfe an houre, or
thereabout, they will grow whitish on the top; let
them yet remaine without stirring, till the upper-
most of them bee fully dried: then stirre them
together, and leave them about one other halfe
houre; and if you finde them dry in the top, stirre
them together againe, and so continue this worke
until they bee thorowly dried; then put them hot
as they are into an earthen pot having a narrow
mouth, and being well leaded within (the Re-
finers of gold and silver call these pots Hookers)
stop it with corke and wet parchment, or with
wax and rosin mixed together and hang your pot
in a chimney, or neare a continuall fire, and so
they will keepe exceeding faire in colour and

most delicate in scent. And it you feare their relenting, take the Rose leaves about Candlemas,
and put them once againe into a sieve, stirring
them up and downe often till they be dry: and
then put them againe hot into your pots.   Sir
Hugh Platt. *Delights for Ladies* 1594.

## ANOTHER WAY FOR THE DRYING OF ROSE LEAVES

DRY them in the heat of a hott sunny day upon a
lead, turning them up and downe till they be dry
(as they do say) then put them up into glasses well
stopt and luted, keeping your glasses in warme
places; and thus you may keepe all flowers; but
herbs after they are dried in this manner, are, best
kept in paper bags, placing the in bags close cupboards.—Sir Hugh Platt. *Delights for Ladies* 1594.

## ROSES AND GILLYFLOWERS KEPT LONG

COVER a Rose that is fresh and in the bud, and

43

gathered in a faire day after the dew is ascended, with the whites of egges well beaten, and presently strew thereon the fine powder of searced sugar, and put them up in luted pots setting the pots in a coole place in sand or gravell: with a fillip at any time you may shake off this inclosure. —Sir Hugh Platt. *Delights for Ladies* 1594.

## TO DRY OR KEEP ROSES

TAKE the Buds of Damask Roses before they are fully blown, pull the leaves and lay them on Boards, in a Room where the heat of the Sun may not come at them; when they are pretty dry, let a large Still be made warm, and lay them on the Top of it till they are crisp; but let them not lie so long as to change their Colour. Then spread them thin; and when they are thoroughly dried, press them down into a Earthen Pan, and keep close covered.—John Nott. *The Receipt Book of John Nott. Cook to the Duke of Bolton* 1723.

44

## TO MAKE ROSE BEADS FOR A ROSARY

GATHER the Roses on a dry day and chop the petals very finely. Put them in a saucepan and barely cover with water. Heat for about an hour but do not let the mixture boil. Repeat this process for the three days and if necessary add more water. The deep black beads made from rose petals are made this rich colour by warming in a rusty pan. It is important never to let the mixture boil but each day to warm it to a moderate heat. Make the beads by working the pulp with the fingers into balls. When thoroughly well worked and fairly dry press on to a bodkin to make the holes in the centres of the beads. Until they are perfectly dry the beads have to be moved frequently on the bodkin or they will be difficult to remove without breaking them. Held for a few moments in a warm hand these heads give out a pleasing fragrance.—Nineteenth century recipe.

# PERFUMES AND SWEET WATERS

## KING EDWARD VI's PERFUME

TAKE twelve spoonfulls of right red rose-water, the weight of six pence in fine powder of sugar, and boyl it on hot Embers and coals softly and the house will smell as though it were full of Roses, but you must burn the Sweet Cypress wood before to take away the gross ayre.—The Queen's Closet Opened by W. M. Cook to Queen Henrietta Maria 1655.

## AN ODORIFEROUS PARFUME FOR CHAMBERS

TAKE a glasseful of Rose Water, Cloves well beaten to powder, a penny weight: then take the fire panne and make it red hot in the fyre, and put thereon of the said Rose water with the sayd pouder of Cloves making it so consume, by little and little but the rose water must be muskt, and you shall make a parfume of excellent good odour.—*A Queens Delight* 1662.

## TO MAKE PERFUMES TO BURN

TAKE half a pound of Damask Rose-buds (the whites cut off) Benjamin three ounces beaten to powder, half a quarter of an ounce of Musk and as much of Ambergris, the like of Civet. Beat all these together in a stone Mortar, then put in an ounce of Sugar, and make it up in Cakes and dry them by the fire.—Sir Kenelm Digby. *Receipts in Physick and Chirurgery* 1668.

## TO MAKE COURT PERFUMES

TAKE three ounces of Benjamin, lay it all night in Damask Rose buds cut clean from the whites, beat them very fine in a stone Mortar till it come to a paste, then take it out and mix it with a dram of Musk finely beaten, as much Civet, mould them up with a little searced Sugar and dry them very well and keep them to burn, one at a time is sufficient.—*The Toilet of Flora.*

## ROSE PASTILLS TO BURN

TAKE Benjamin three ounces, storax two ounces,
Damask Rose-buds one ounce; grind the Roses
by themselves, and the rest also: Then take Lignum Aloes, Amber, fine Sugar, Civet, powder of
Cypress, half a quarter of a pound; grind these
well together. Then mix it with gum Tragacanth
dissolved in Orange-flowers or Rose-water and
make them up.—Sir Kenelm Digby. *Choice and
Experimented Receipts* 1668.

## TO MAKE AN EXCELLENT PERFUME

TAKE half a pound of Damask Rose Buds cut clear
from the whites, stamp them well, and add to
them two large spoonfuls of Damask Rose-water,
put them into a Bottle, stop them close, let them
stand all night, then take two ounces and a half of
Benjamin beat it fine, add twenty grains of Musk
and (if you please) as much Civet, mingle these
with the Roses, beating all well together, make

it up in little Cakes, and dry them between Sheets of Paper.—*The Receipt Book of Charles Carter. Cook to the Duke of Argyll 1732.*

### A SWEET WATER

TAKE a gallon of Spring water, 3 handfulls of roses, a handfull of Lavender flowers, as much sweet marjoram, the pelling of six oringes, 12 cloves, bruise all these and put to them one ounce of orrice powder, 4 ounce of benjamin. Put all these into a rose still and draw off the first quart by itselfe and then a pint, you may draw after that another water from the lees which serve for present use but not keep, put into your quart bottle 12 pennyworth of musk, and in the pint bottle 6 pennyworth tied in bags and a little juniper sliced very thin as much as will lay on half a crown, 2 or 3 spoonfulls will sweeten a bason of water: keep it stop't very close: it will keep a year or 2.—*The Book of Simples circa 1650.*

52

## MUSK ROSE WATER

TAKE two handfuls of your Musk Rose leaves, put them into about a quart of fair water and a quarter of a pound of sugar, let this stand and steep about half an hour, then take your water and flowers and pour them out of one vessel into another till such time as the water hath taken the scent and taste of the flowers, then set it in a cool place a-cooling and you will find it a most excellent scent-water.—William Rabisha. *The Whole Body of Cookery Dissected* 1675.

## AN EXCELLENT WATER FOR THE HEAD AND FOR SLEEP CALLED YE EMPEROUR CHARLESES WATER

WHEN roses are blown, take a quart of good aquavitae in a glass with a narrow neck and when the roses are half blown take a handfull of the leaves without ye seed, put them into the glass and when the marjoram bloweth and the Apiastrum, take then a handfull of their buds, chop

them small and put them into the glass. Take also Cloves, Nutmegs, Cinnamon, Mace, Cardamum, of these an ounce and a half: bruise all these grossly and put it in the glass and when the lavender and rosemary are blown add a handfull of these flowers also, shake them well together and stop it close: let it stand 10 days in a hot sun: it must be used by anointing the temples and nostrells; it fortifieth and corroborateth the head and memory.—*The Book of Simples circa.* 1650.

## TO MAKE ROSE-WATER

TO make an excellent Rose-water, let the flowers be gathered two or three hours after sun-rising in very fine weather; beat them in a marble mortar into a paste, and leave them in the mortar soaking in their juice for five or six hours; then put the mass into a coarse canvas bag, and press out the juice to every quart of which add a pound of fresh Damask Roses, and let them stand in infusion for twenty four hours. Then put the whole into a

54

glass alembic, lute on a head of receiver, and place it on sand heat. Distil at first with a gentle fire, which is to be encreased gradually till the drops follow each other as quick as possible; draw off the water as long as it continues to run clear, then put out the fire, and let the alembic stand till cold. The distilled water at first will have very little fragrancy, but after being exposed to the heat of the sun about eight days, in a bottle lightly stopped with a bit of paper, it acquires an admirable scent.—*The Toilet of Flora*.

## TO MAKE A RARE SWEET WATER

TAKE sweet Marjoram, Damask Roses, Lavender, Rosemary, Maudlin, Balm, Thyme, Walnut Leaves, Pinks, of all a like quantity enough to fill your still, then take of the best Orrice powder, Damask Rose powder and Storax, of each two ounces; strew one handful or two of your Powders upon the Herbs, then distill them with a soft fire; tie a little musk in a piece of lawn and hang

it in the Glass wherein it drops, and when it is all drawn out, take your sweet cakes and mix them with the powders which are left, and lay them among your clothes or with sweet Oyles, and burn them for perfume.—*A Queen's Delight* 1662.

## TO MAKE A SPECIALL SWEET WATER TO PERFUME CLOTHES IN THE FOLDING BEING WASHED

TAKE a quart of Damask rose water and put it into a glasse, put unto it a handfull of Lavender flowers, two ounces of Orris, a dram of Muske, the weight of four pence of Amber-greece, as much Civet, foure drops of Oyle of Cloves, stop this close, and set it in the Sunne a fortnight; put one spoonfull of this water into a bason of common water and put it into a glasse and so sprinkle your clothes therewith in your folding: the dregs left in the bottome (when the water is spent) will make as much more, if you keepe them, and

56

put fresh Rose-water to it.—Sir Hugh Platt.
*Delights for Ladies* 1594.

## TO MAKE SWEET WATER OF THE BEST KIND

TAKE a thousand Damask Roses, two good hand-fuls of Lavender tops, a three-penny weight of Mace, two ounces of Cloves bruised, a quart of running water; put a little water into the bottom of an earthen pot and then put in your Roses and Lavender, with the Spices by little and little, and in the putting in, always knead them down with your fist, and so continue it untill you have wrought up all your Roses and Lavender and in the working put in always a little of your water: then put in your pot close and let it stand in four dayes, in which time every morning and evening put in your hand and pull from the bottom of your pot the said Roses, working it for a time, and then distill it, and having in the glass of water a grain or two of Musk wrapt up in a piece of Sarcenet or fine cloth.—Ibid.

## TO PERFUME GLOVES

TAKE Rose-water and Angelica-water, and put to them the powder of Cloves, Ambergreece, Musk and Lignum Aloes, Benjamin and Calamus aromaticus: boyl then hang them in the Sun to dry and turn them often: and thus three times wet them and dry them again: or otherwise take Rose-water and wet your Gloves therein, then hang them up till they be almost dry; then take half an ounce of Benjamin, and grind it with the oyl of Almonds, and rub it on the Gloves till it be almost dryed in: then take twenty grains of Musk, and grind them together with oyl of Almonds and so rub it on the Gloves and then hang them up to dry, or let them dry in your bosome, and so after use them at your pleasure.—Gervase Markham. *The English Housewife* 1675.

## A VERY RARE AND PLEASANT DAMASK-WATER

TAKE a quart of Malmsey lees, or a quart of Malm-

58

sey simply, damask Rose-leaves four handfuls,
and as many of Red, one handful of Marjerom, of
Basil as much, of Lavender four handfuls, Bay
leaves one good handful, the peels of six Oranges,
or four want of them one handful of the tender
leaves of Wallnut leaves, of Benjamin half an
ounce, of Calamus Aramaticus as much, of Camo-
hire four drams, of Cloves one ounce, then take a
pottle of running water and put in all these spices
bruised into your water and Malmsey together,
in a close stopped pot with a good handful of
Rosemary, and let them stand for the space of six
dayes: then distill it with a soft fire: then set it in
the Sun sixteen dayes with four grains of Musk
bruised. This quantity will make three quarts of
water.—Gervase Markham. *The English House-
Wife* 1675.


## TO MAKE SWEET WATER

TAKE Damask Roses at discretion, Basil, sweet
Marjoram, Lavender, Wall-nut leafs, of each two

*Rosa*

handfulls, Rosemary one handful, a little Balm,
Cloves Cinnamon, Bay-leafs, Limon and Orange
pills of each a few; pour upon these as much white
wine as will conveniently wet them and let them
infuse ten or twelve days: then distill it off.—
Sir Kenelm Digby. *Choice and Experimented Receipts* 1668.

## WATER FOR THE CASTYING GLASSE

PUT into some little vessell of Silver, a little Rose
water made with Muske, and a little Civet, and
Cloves, and Styrax. Mix them and perfume any
clothes with the vapour or the smoke thereof, it
is a marvellous sweet savoure, if thou wilt keep
close the vessell diligently and when thou think-
est good, put more Rose water unto it, that it
maye be renewed.—Bullein's *Bulwark of defence* . .
which Bulwarke is kepte with Hillarius the Gar-
diner 1562.

## ROSE WATER

SOME do put rose water in a glass and they put

roses with their dew thereto and they make it to
boile in water, then they set it in the sune tyll it
be readde and this water is beste.

Also drye roses put to the nose to smell do com-
forte the braine and the harte and quencheth
sprites.—Askham's *Herbal* 1550.

## TO MAKE THE SWEET WATER, THE BEST, CALLED IN FRENCH L' EAU D'ANGE

TAKE three pints of Rose-water, half a pint of
Orange-flower-water, Musk, Ambergris, Lignum
Aloes, twenty five grains, Civet fifteen grains,
Benjamin four ounces, Storax one ounce, all in
fine powder; mix all these well together, and put
them in a Brass-pot, covering it very close with
Linen, and set it to boil in a kettle full of water
the space of three hours; then pour off the clear,
and put upon the remaining matter the same
quantity of fresh Rose and Orange-flower water,
and five or six grains of Civet, then of the rest
you make Pastils or Cassolettes.—The Closet of
Sir Kenelm Digby Opened 1669.

61

## METHOD OF SCENTING SNUFF

THE Flowers that most readily communicat their flavour to Snuff are Orange Flowers, Muck Roses, Jasmine, and Tuberoses. You must procure a box lined with dry white paper; in this strow your Snuff on the bottom about the thickness of an inch, over which place a thin layer of Flowers, then another layer of Snuff, and continue to lay your Flowers and Snuff alternately in this manner, until the box is full. After they have lain together four and twenty hours, sift your Snuff through a sieve to separate it from the Flowers, which are to be thrown away, and fresh ones applied in their room in the former method. Continue to do this till the Snuff is sufficiently scented; then put it into a canister, which keep close stopped.—*The Country Lady's Director* 1732.

## ODORIFEROUS CANDLES AGAINST VENOME AND THE PLAGUE

TAKE red Roses, Cloves of each three ounces,

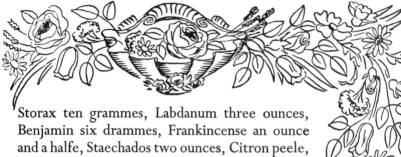

Storax ten grammes, Labdanum three ounces,
Benjamin six drammes, Frankincense an ounce
and a halfe, Staechados two ounces, Citron peele,
Yellow Sanders, of each three drammes, Juniper
berries halfe an ounce, Musk and Ambergreese
of each halfe a scruple: forme them into Candles
with gumdragant dissolved in Rose water.—*The
Charitable Physitian* by Philbert Guibert Phisytian
Regent in Paris 1639.

# CULINARY RECIPES

## ROSE PETAL CONSERVE

*Ingredients:* Red Rose Petals; Sugar; Orange Flower water.

*Method.* Red roses make the best conserve and they must be gathered when fully open but before they begin to fade. Cut off the white heels for these have a bitter flavour. Dry the petals on sieves out of direct sunlight and if possible in a draught as then they dry quickly. When dried put a pound of petals into a muslin bag and plunge for a moment into boiling water. Drain well. Have ready a syrup made with a pound of loaf sugar and very little water. Add two table-spoons of orange flower water. Put in the petals and cook until the conseve is very thick. Keep on pressing the petals under the syrup. Pour into small jars and cover down securely as for jam.

This conserve has a most delicious flavour and the more richly scented the roses the better the flavour. Etoile de Hollande, General McArthur and other deep red scented roses are the best to use.

## ROSE PETAL JELLY

*Ingredients:* Dried Rose Petals; Apples; Preserving sugar.

*Method.* Make apply jelly with good cooking Apples but do not peel them. Cut them up fairly small, put them in a preserving pan and cover with cold water. Simmer slowly to a pulp. Strain the pulp through a jelly bag and leave to drip all night. Measure the liquid and to every pint allow a pound of preserving sugar. Stir until the sugar is dissolved and then put in as many dried rose petals as the liquor will hold. Boil till the jelly sets when tested on a cold plate. Strain before potting.

## SAUCE EGLANTINE

THIS sauce which is excellent to serve with roast mutton, etc., was frequently made at Balmoral in Queen Victoria's time.

*Ingredients:* Sweet Briar Hips; Lemon Juice.

*Method.* Remove all the seeds from the hips and

then make a purée of them with as little water as possible. Sweeten to taste and add a little lemon juice.

### ROSE HIP MARMALADE

*Ingredients:* Wild rose hips; Sugar.
*Method.* To every pound of Rose hips allow half a pint of water. Boil till the fruit is tender. Pass the pulp through a sieve fine enough to keep back the seeds. To each pound of pulp allow a pound of preserving sugar. Boil till it jellies.

### TO MAKE A CAKE WITH ROSE WATER, THE WAY OF THE ROYAL PRINCESS, THE LADY ELIZABETH, DAUGHTER TO KING CHARLES THE FIRST

TAKE halfe a pecke of flowre, half a pinte of rose water, a pint of ale yeast, a pint of creame. A pound and a half of butter six egges (leaves out the whites) four pounds of currants, one half pound of sugar, one nutmeg and a little salt.

Work it very well and let it stand half an hour by the fire and then work it again and then make it up and let it stand an hour and a halfe in the oven; let not your oven be too hot.—*The Queen's Closet Opened*. By W. M. Cook to Queen Henrietta Maria.

## TO MAKE A CONSERVE OF ROSE HIPS

GATHER the hips before they grow soft, cut off the heads and stalks, slit them in halves, and take out all the seeds and white that is in them very clean; then put in an earthen pan, and stir them every day else they will grow mouldy; let them stand till they are soft enough to rub through a coarse hair sieve; as the pulp comes take it off the sieve; they are a dry berry; will require pains to rub it through; then add its weight in sugar, and mix it well together without boiling; keeping it in deep gallipots for use.—E. Smith. *The Complete Housewife* 1736.

## CONSERVE OF ROSES, VIOLETS, COWSLIPS, OR MARIGOLDS

TAKE red rose-buds, clip all the white, either bruised or withered from them; then add to every pound of roses three pounds of sugar, stamp the roses very small, putting to them a little juice of lemons or rose water as they become dry; when you think your roses small enough then put your sugar to them so beat them together till they be well mingled, then put it up in gallipots or glasses.

In this manner is made the conserve of flowers of violets, which both cool and open in a burning fever or ague, being dissolved in almond milk and so taken; and excellent good for any inflammation in children.

Thus you may also make conserve of cowslips, which strengthens the brain and is a preservative against madness, it helps the memory, assuaget the pain of the head and helpeth most infirmites thereof.

In like manner you may also make conseve of

marigolds which taken fasting in the morning is
very good against melancholy.—Mrs. Woolley.
*The Gentlewoman's Companion* 1673.

## TO MAKE ROSE-DROPS

THE roses and sugar must be beat separately into
a very fine powder, and both sifted; to a pound of
sugar an ounce of red roses, they must be mixed
together, and then wet with as much juice of
Lemon as will make it into a stiff paste; set it on
a slow fire in a silver porringer, and stir it well;
and when it is scalding hot quite through take it
off and drop in small portions on a paper; set
them near the fire, the next day they will come
off.—E. Smith. *The Complete Housewife* 1736.

## SUGAR OF ROSES IN VARIOUS
## FIGURES

CLIP off the white of rose-buds, and dry them in
the sun. Having finely pounded an ounce of them,
take a pound of loaf sugar  Wet the sugar in rose

72

water, and boil to a candy height. Put in your powder of roses and the juice of lemon. Mix all well together, put it on a pie plate, and put it into lozenges, or make it into any figure you fancy, such as men, women or birds. If you want ornaments for your desert, you may gild or colour them to your liking.—*The London Art of Cookery* by John Farley Principal Cook at the London Tavern 1804.

## CONSERVE OF ROSES

TAKE buds of red Roses somewhat they be ready to spread; cut the red part of the leaves from the white, and beate and grinde them in a stone mortar with a pestle of wood and to every ounce of roses, put three ounces of sugar in the grinding (after the leaves are well beaten) and grinde them together till they be perfectly incorporated, then put in a glasse made of purpose, or else into an earthen pot, stop it close and so keepe it. Thus you may make conserves of all kindes of flowers

73

commonly used for conserves.—John Partridge.
*Treasurey of Hidden Secrets & Commodious Conceits*
1586.

## TO MAKE SUGAR OF ROSES

TAKE the deepest-coloured red Roses, pick
them, cut off the white buttons and dry your red
leaves in an oven, till they be as dry as possible:
then beat them to powder and searse them, then
take halfe a pound of sugar beaten fine, put it
into your pan with as much fair water as will wet
it, then set it in a chafing dish of coals and let it
boyle till it be sugar again; then put as much
powder of the Roses as will make it look very
red, stir them well together, and when it is
thoroughly cold, put in boxes.—Sir Hugh Platt.
*Delights for Ladies* 1594.

## PICKLED ROSEBUDS

PICK rosebuds and put them in an earthen pipkin,
with white wine vinegar and sugar and so you

may use cowslips, violets or rosemary flowers.—
Murrell's *Two Books of Cookeries & Carving* 1650.

## TO MAKE A TART OF HIPS

TAKE hips, cut them and take out the seeds very
clean, then wash them and season them with
sugar, cinnamon and ginger, close the tart, bake
it scrape on sugar and serve it in.—*The Art and
Mystery of Cookery Approved by the Fifty-five Years
Experience and Industry of Robert May* 1671.

## MARMALADE FROM ROSE HIPS

TO every pound of hips allow half a pint of water;
boil till the fruit is tender, then pass the pulp
through a sieve which will keep back the seeds.
To each pound of pulp add one pound of preserving sugar and boil until it jellies.—E. G.
Hayden *Travels Round Our Village.*

## JAM MADE WITH THE BERRIES OF WILD
## DOG ROSES

CHOOSE ripe large sound berries from a dog rose

75

bush (Eglantine). They should be hard. Scrape each berry and cut off tip through opening remove pulp with the aid of a bodkin or tiny spoon, being careful not to break berry. Tie a piece of linen round the bodkin or little spoon and wipe the inside to remove any pulp that may remain. There are fine hairs which must be removed. Drop berries into cold water and rinse several times shaking about to make sure that all little hairs are gone. Put into a saucepan, pour over boiling water, put on fire and as soon as the water boils again pour berries out on a sieve and pour cold water over them, Then put a clean cloth over the sieve and put each berry standing with the little hole underneath to drain well.

Prepare syrup. For every pound of berries use 3 lb. sugar and 23/4 2 and 3/4 cups water. Let it boil twice then put in berries and cook till tender. Remove scum which forms on jam. When tender pour into china bowl, tie a cloth over and let stand for several days. Every now and then move the bowl about, so that the

76

berries are well filled with the syrup. Pour into jars and close with air-tight stoppers or parchment paper. Keep in a dry place.—*The Russian Cook Book*. Compiled and translated by Princess Alexandre Gazarene 1924.

### WILD ROSE OR DOG ROSE JAM

SORT out $\frac{1}{2}$ lb rose petals (dog roses are best) cut off all yellow or damaged bits, put into boiling water and boil well, then pour on to a sieve to drain. Dry petals on a clean napkin and put on dish. Powder with $\frac{1}{2}$ lb sifted sugar.

Make syrup with $1\frac{1}{2}$ lb sugar and $\frac{1}{2}$ cup water. When thick pour into it juice of $\frac{1}{2}$ lemon and put in rose petals. Boil once. Pour into china bowl. When cold add 1 drop attar of roses. Mix well and pour into jars.—*The Russian Cook Book*, compiled and translated by Princess Alexandre Gazarine 1924.

77

## ROSE-WATER AND ROSE-VINEGAR OF THE COLOUR OF THE ROSE, AND OF THE COWSLIP AND VIOLET VINEGAR

IF you would make your Rose-water and Rose-vinegar of a rubie colour then make choice of the crimson-velvet coloured leaves, clipping away the whites with a pair of sheares: and being thorow dryed, put a good large handfull of them into a pint of Damask or red Rose-water; stop your glasse well, and set it in the sunne, till you see that the leaves have lost their colour or for more expedition, you may performe this worke *in balneo* in a few houres; and when you take out the old leaves you may put in fresh, till you finde the colour to please you. Keepe this Rose-water in the glassess very well stopt; the fuller the better. What I have said of Rose-water, the same may also be intended of Rose-vinegar, violet, marigold and cowslip vinegar; but the whiter vinegar chuse for this purpose, the colour thereof will be the brighter, and therefore distilled

78

vinegar is best for this purpose.—Sir Hugh Platt.
*Delights for Ladies* 1594.

## TO MAKE VINEGAR OF ROSES

IN summer time when roses blow, gather them,
ere they be full sized or blown out, and in dry
weather plucke the leaves, let them lie halfe a
daye upon a faire boord, then have a vessell with
vinegar of one or two gallons (if you will make so
much roset) put there in a great quantity of the
said leaves, stop the vessell close after that ye
have stirred them well together; let it stand a day
and a night, then divide your vinegar and rose
leaves together in two parts, put them in two
great glasses, and put in rose-leaves enough; stop
the glasses close, set them upon a shelfe under a
wall side on the south side without your house
where the sunne may come to them the most part
of the day; let them stand there the whole summer long, and then straine the vinegar from the
Roses, and keep the leaves and put in new leaves

79

of halfe a daies gathering, the vinegar will have the more odour of the Rose.

You may use instead of vinegar, wine, that it may wax eager and receive the virtue of the Roses both at once.

Moreover you may make your vinegar of wine, white, red, or claret; but the red rose is astringent, and the white is laxative. Also the Damask Rose is not so great a binder as the red Rose and the white looseth most of all: Hereof you may make Vinegar roset.

Then also you may make vinegar of violets or of elderne flowers but you must first gather and use your flowers of elderne, as they shall be shewed hereafter, when we speake of making conserve of elderne flowers.—John Partridge. *The Treasurie of Hidden Secrets & Commodious Conceits* 1586.

## A WHITE LEACH

TAKE six table spoonfuls of Rose water, two drops

of oil of Mace, two grains of Musk. Warm together sufficiently to melt four ounces of Ising-glass. When the Ising-glass is melted strain through a jelly bag. When cold cut in slices and serve with cream.—Recipe dated 1890.

## TO MAKE WAFERS

PUT the yolks of four eggs, and three spoonfuls of Rose-water to a quart of flour; mingle them well, make them into a batter with cream and double-refined sugar, pour it on very thin, and bake it on Irons.—John Nott. *The Receipt Book of John Nott, Cook to the Duke of Bolton* 1723.

## ROSE AND FRUIT SALAD

COVER the bottom of the dish in which this sweet is to be served with red and pink Rose petals. Mash four very ripe Bananas and with them mix an equal quantity of finely chopped Dates. Put

F                81

this mixture in a layer on the rose petals and cover the mixture thickly with Rose petal conserve. Just before serving pour gently the juice of two oranges over the conserve and then cover with a thick layer of clotted cream. Decorate with crystallised Rose petals. The dish should be so arranged that the Rose petals show well all round the sweetmeat served on them.

## TO CANDY ROSE LEAVES AS NATURAL AS IF THEY GREW ON TREES

TAKE of your fairest Rose leaves, Red or Damask, and on a sunshine day sprinkle them with Rosewater, lay them on one by one on a fair paper, then take some double refined sugar beaten very fine, put it in a fine lawn searse when you have laid abroad all the rose leaves in the hottest of the sun, searse sugar thinly all over them and anon the sun will candie the sugar; then turn the leaves and searse sugar on the other side, and

turn them often in the sun, sometimes sprinkling
Rose-water and sometimes searsing sugar on
them, until they be enough, and come to your
liking and being thus done you may keep them.—
William Rabisha. *The Whole Body of Cookery Dissected* 1675.

## HOW TO PRESERVE WHOLE ROSES, GILLYFLOWERS, MARIGOLDS, ETC.

DIP a rose that is neither in the bud, nor over-
blowne in a sirup, consisting of sugar, double refined, and Rose-water boiled to his full height,
then open the leaves one by one with a fine
smooth bodkin either of bone or wood; and presently if it be a hot sunny day, and whilest the
sunne is in some good height, lay them on papers
in the sunne, or else dry them with some gentle
heat in a close roome, heating the room before
you set them in, or in an oven upon papers, in
pewter dishes, and then put them up in glasses;
and keepe them in dry cupboards neere the fire:

83

you must take out the seeds, if you meane to eat them. You may proove this preserving with sugar-candy instead of sugar if you please.—Sir Hugh Platt. *Delights for Ladies* 1594.

## THE OIL COMMONLY CALLED THE SPIRIT OF ROSES

TAKE of Damask, or Red Roses, being fresh, as many as you please, infuse them in as much warm water as is sufficient for the space of twenty four houres; then strain, and press them, and repeat the infusion severall times with pressing, until the liquor become fully impregnated, which then must be distilled in an Alembick with a refrigerator, let the Spirit which swims on the Water be separated and the water kept for a new infusion.

This kind of Spirit may be made by bruising the Roses with Salt, or laying a laye of Roses, and another of Salt, and so keeping them half a year or more, which then must be distilled in as much common water or Rose water as is sufficient.— John French. *The Art of Distillation* 1652.

84

## TO MAKE OYLE OF ROSES

TAKE of oyle eighteen ounces, the buds of Roses (the white ends of them cut away) three ounces, lay the Roses abroad in the shadow four and twenty houres, then put them in a glasse to the oyle, and stop the glass close; and set it in the sunne at least forty dayes.—John Partridge. *The Treasurie of Hidden Secrets and Commodious Conceits* 1586.

## TO MAKE OYLE OF ROSES THREE WAYES

THE first way is, take a pound of red Rose buds, beat them in a marble morter with a woodden pestle, then put them into an earthen pot, and poure upon the foure pound of oyle of olives, letting them infuse the space of a moneth in the Sunne, or in the chimney corner stirring of them sometimes, then heate it, 'and presse it and straine it, and put it into the same pot or other vessell to keepe.

The second is, take halfe a pound of red Roses,

85

and halfe a pound of Damaske roses, beate them together in a marble morter, and put them into a pot, and poure upon them foure pound of oyle, and let them infuse the space of twelve houres, then pour them all into a pan and boyle them two or three boylings, and straine them and presse them in a strong towell in the presse and in the meane time put in the pot as many more Roses and poure the oyle upon them and so beate them and presse them and put Roses to the oyle three times and then boyle it until all the humidity bee consumed. The third is to take all Damask roses and no red and make three infusions as before.—
*The Charitable Physitian* by Philbert Guibert Esq., & Physitian Regent in Paris 1639.


## A PERFUME TO PERFUME ANY SORT OF CONFECTIONS

TAKE musk, the like quantity of Oil of Nutmeg, infuse them in Rose-water, and with it sprinkle your Banqueting preparations and the scent will

86

be as pleasing as the taste.—*England's newest way in all sorts of Cookery*, by Henry Howard, Free Cook of London 1710.

## TO MAKE ROSSOLY THE ITALIAN WAY

GATHER fresh Damask Roses, Orange Flowers, Jessamy Flowers, Cloves and Gillyflowers; pick them clean, set on some water to boil, when it has boiled well let it stand to cool a little; put these clean Flowers into a China Bason, pour the water upon them when it is not hotter than to bear the finger in it; then cover it up, and let it stand Three Hours, gently pour all into a fine Linen Bag, and let the Water run off without squeezing the Flowers to a pint of this Water, add a quart of fine Melasses Spirit, and halfe a Pint of strong cinnamon water: add three teaspoons of Essence of Ambergrease, and stir all well together. This is the true Rossoly.—*The Receipt Book of Elizabeth Cleland* 1759.

87

## ROSE WINE

TAKE a well glazed earthen vessel and put into it three gallons of rose-water drawn with a cold still. Put into that a sufficient quantity of rose leaves cover it close, and set it for an hour in a kettle or copper of hot water, to take out the whole strength and tincture of the roses; and when it be cold press the rose leaves hard into the liquor, and steep fresh ones in it, repeating it till the liquor has got the full strength of the roses. To every gallon of liquor put three pounds of loaf sugar, and stir it well, that it may melt and disperse in every part. Then put it into a cask, or other convenient vessel, to ferment, and put into it a piece of bread toasted hard and covered with yeast. Let it stand about thirty days, when it will be ripe and have a fine flavour, having the whole strength and scent of the roses in it; and you may greatly improve it by adding to it wine and spices. By this method of infusion, wine of carnations, clove gilliflowers, violets, primroses, or any other flower, having a curious scent, may

88

be made.—*The London Art of Cookery* by John Farley Principal Cook at the London Tavern 1804.

## TO MAKE A SIROP OF ROSES OR VIOLETS

TAKE of violets or roses a pounde, steepe them in three pints of warme water, put it in an earthen pot with a narrow mouth the space of seven houres or more. AFTER straine it and warme the water againe and put in againe so many Roses or Violets, and likewise let them lye in steepe eight hours, and thus do at the least five times, the oftener the better, in especiall the roses, and after take to every pint a pounde of sugar and steepe them together, till the sugar be molten, then seethe them together with a soft sweet fire to ght height of a Sirrup; if you have more Roses or Violets, or fewer and let so much be the proportion of the water, according to the proportion before.—*The Good Housewife's Handmaid* 1585.

## A SINGULAR MANNER OF MAKING THE
## SIRUP OF ROSES

FILL a silver bason three quarters full of rain
water or Rose water, put therein a convenient
proportion of Rose leaves; cover the bason and
set it upon a pot of hot water (as we usually bake
a custard) in three quarters of an houre, or one
whole houre at the most, you shall purchase the
whole strength and tincture of the Roses: then
take out those leaves wringing out all their
liquor gently, and steepe more fresh leaves in the
same water: continue this iteration seven times,
and then make it up in a sirup; and this sirup
worketh more kindely than that which is made
meerly of the juice of the Rose. You may make
sundry other sirups in this manner.—Sir Hugh
Platt. *Delights for Ladies* 1594.

## HONEY OF ROSES

CUT the white heels from Red Roses, take halfe a
pound of them and put them into a stone jar, and

pour on them three pints of boiling water. Stir well and let them stand twelve hours. Then press off the liquor and when it has settled add to it five pounds of honey. Boil it well, and when it is of the consistence of a thick syrup it is ready to put away.—Thomas Tryon. *A Treatise of Cleanness in Meates* 1692.

## HONEY OF ROSES

TAKE four ounces of dried red Rose petals the white heels cut off before they were dried, three pints of boiling water and five pounds of honey. Pour the boiling water on to the dried Rose petals and leave for six hours. Strain and add the honey. Boil to a thick consistency.—Nineteenth century recipe.

## TO MAKE A CONSERVE OF ROSES BOILED

TAKE a quart of red Rose water, a quart of fair water, boil in the water a pound of red rose

leaves, the whites cut off, the leaves must be oiled very tender; then take three pounds of sugar, put to it a pound at a time, and let it boil a little between every pound, so put it up in your pots.—*A Queen's Delight* 1695.

## TO MAKE CONSERVE OF RED ROSES

LET your Roses be gathered before they are quite blown, pound them in a stone mortar, and add to them twice their weight in double-refined sugar and put them into a glass close stopt up but do not fill it full. Let them stand three months before you use them, remembring to stir them once a Day.—John Nott. *The Receipt Book of John Nott. Cook to the Duke of Bolton* 1723.

## TO MAKE CONSERVE OF ROSES
## UNBOILED

TAKE a pound of red rose leaves, the whites cut

off, stamp them very fine, take a pound of sugar and beat it with the roses and put it in a pot and cover it with leather and set it in a cool place.— *A Queen's Delight* 1695.

## CONSERVE OF RED ROSES

DOCTOR GLISSON makes his conserve of red roses thus: Boil gently a pound of red Rose-leaves in about a pint and a halfe (or a little more as by discretion you shall find fit, after having done it once; the Doctor's apothcary takes two pints) of Spring water: till the water have drawn out all the Tincture of the Roses in to it self and that the leaves be very tender and looke pale like Linnen; which may be in good halfe hour, or an hour keeping the pot covered while it boileth. Then pour the tincted Liquor from the pale leaves, strain it out, pressing it gently, so that you may have liquor enough to dissolve our sugar, and set it upon the fire by it self to boil, putting into it a pound of pure double-refined sugar in small

93

powder; which as soon as it is dissolved put in a
second pound; then a third, lastly a fourth, so
that you have four pounds of sugar to every pound
of Rose leaves, (the Apothecary useth to put all
the four pounds into the Liquor together at
once). Boil these four pounds of sugar with the
tincted Liquor till it be a high syrup, very near a
candy height (as high as it can be not to flake or
candy) Then put the pale rose-leaves into this
high syrup as it yet standeth upon the fire, or
immediately upon the taking it off the fire. But
predently take it off from the fire, and stir them
exceedling well together to mix them uniformly;
then let them stand till they be cold, then pot
them up. If you put up your Conserve into pots,
while it is yet thoroughly warm, and leave them
uncovered some days, putting them in the hot
sun or stove, there will grow a fine candy upon
the top which will preserve the conserve with
paper upon it from moulding till you break the
candied crust, to take out some of the conserve.

The colour both of the Rose leaves and the

94

syrup about them will be exceeding beautiful
and red, and the taste excellent, and the whole
very tender and smoothing and easie to digest in
the stomack without clogging it as doth the
ordinary rough conserve made of raw Roses
beaten with sugar, which is very rough in the
throat.—Sir Kenelm Digby.  *The Closet of Sir
Kenelm Digby Opened* 1669.